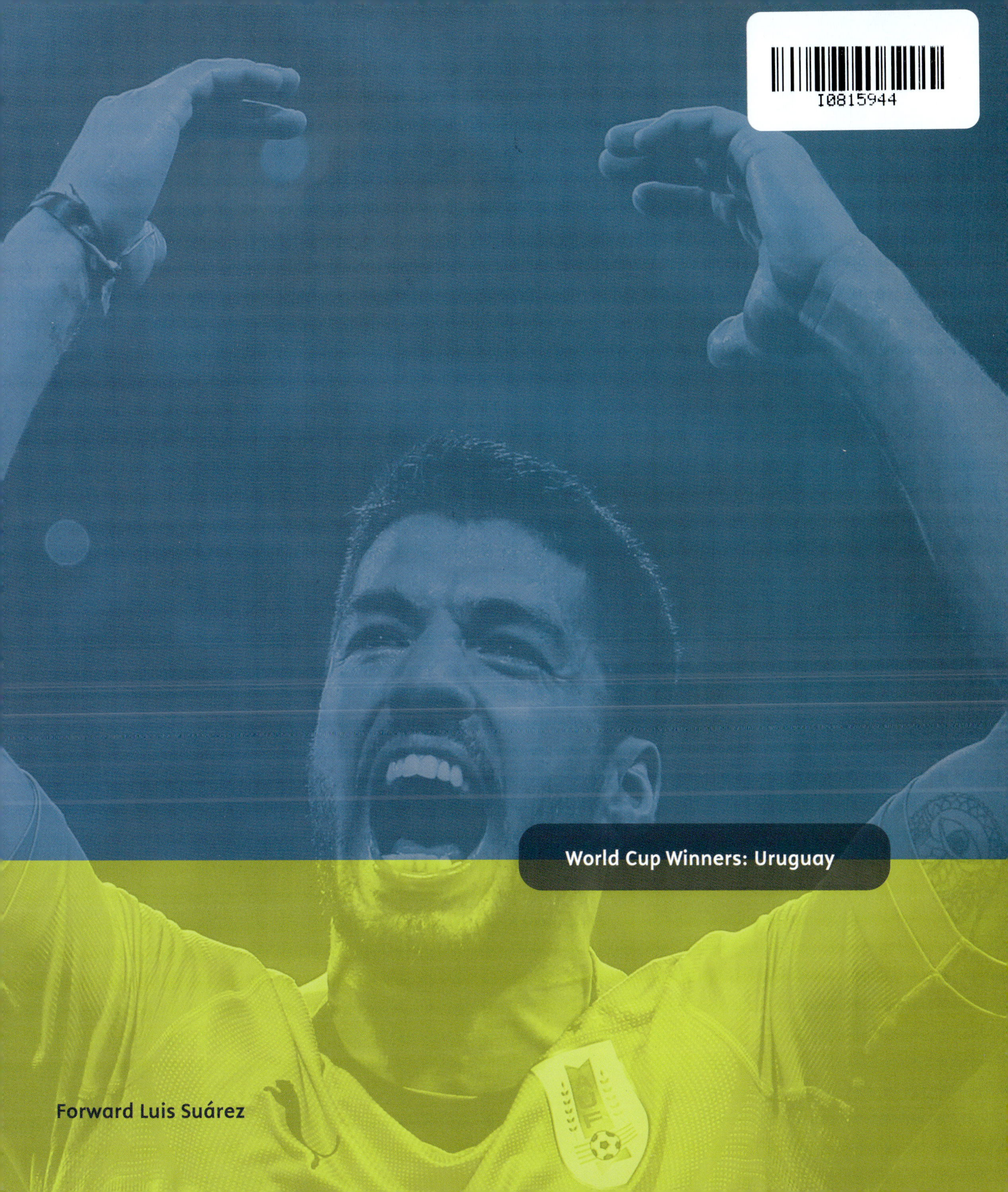
World Cup Winners: Uruguay
Forward Luis Suárez

The 1930 Uruguay national team

WORLD CUP WINNERS

URUGUAY

JAMES BARRY

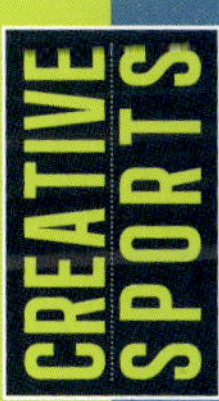

CREATIVE EDUCATION / CREATIVE PAPERBACKS

Published by Creative Education and Creative Paperbacks
P.O. Box 227, Mankato, Minnesota 56002
Creative Education and Creative Paperbacks are imprints
of The Creative Company
www.thecreativecompany.us

Book design by Blue Design (www.bluedes.com)

Images by Getty Images/Anadolu, 15, DANIEL GARCIA, 12, DANTE FERNANDEZ, 4, ElOjoTorpe, 9, Ernesto Ryan, 5, 24, Fox Photos, 6, Lars Baron, 3, 10, ODD ANDERSEN, 1, Visionhaus, cover, 7; IMAGO/ZUMA Press Wire, 16; Wikimedia Commons/Ailura, 20, public domain, 2, 19
Every effort has been made to contact copyright holders for material reproduced in this book. Any omissions will be rectified in subsequent printings if notice is given to the publisher.

Library of Congress Cataloging-in-Publication Data
Names: Barry, James (Author of children's books), author.
Title: Uruguay / James Barry.
Description: Mankato, MN : Creative Education and Creative Paperbacks, 2026. | Series: Creative sports. World Cup winners | Includes index. | Audience: Ages 7–10 | Audience: Grades 2–3 | Summary: "Uruguay defeated mighty Argentina to win the first-ever FIFA World Cup in 1930 and repeated the feat against Brazil 20 years later. This elementary title follows "La Celeste" through thrilling soccer action"– Provided by publisher.
Identifiers: LCCN 2024046143 (print) | LCCN 2024046144 (ebook) | ISBN 9798889896050 (library binding) | ISBN 9781682777718 (paperback) | ISBN 9798889896852 (ebook)
Subjects: LCSH: Soccer—Uruguay–History–Juvenile literature. | World Cup (Soccer)–History–Juvenile literature.
Classification: LCC GV944.U7 B36 2026 (print) | LCC GV944.U7 (ebook) | DDC 796.334/66809895–dc23/eng/20241213
LC record available at https://lccn.loc.gov/2024046143
LC ebook record available at https://lccn.loc.gov/2024046144

Printed in India

Striker Darwin Núñez

Goalkeeper Roque Máspoli

CONTENTS

Home of the Team

Uruguay is a small country in South America. Most of the country is farmland. Farmers raise sheep and cattle. There are more sheep than people in Uruguay.

Uruguayans love to cheer on their national team. It's one of the few teams to have won the World Cup. The World Cup is a worldwide soccer tournament. Countries make teams of their best players. Every four years, they compete to become world champion.

Striker Diego Forlán

Team Traditions

he Uruguay national team is known as "La Celeste" ("The Sky Blue") for its light blue jerseys. The small country takes pride in defeating bigger countries in soccer. Uruguay's greatest **rivals** are its neighbors Argentina and Brazil.

Forward Álvaro Recoba

URUGUAY

The team motto is "Garra Charrúa." It means "Claw of the Charrúa." The Charrúa were a native people in Uruguay. The team often sees itself as the **underdog**. "Garra Charrúa" means it will never give up. It will always try to claw its way to victory.

Team History

In 1924, Uruguay became the first South American soccer team to play in the Olympics. It won every match on its way to a gold medal. Uruguay defended its gold medal in the 1928 Olympics. It defeated Argentina 2–1 in the final. There was no World Cup yet. The first World Cup took place in 1930. Uruguay was chosen as the host country because it had dominated international play.

Uruguay won every match in the first World Cup. La Celeste defeated Argentina 4–2 in the final. Winning the first World Cup completed Uruguay's golden era of soccer. Twenty years later, Uruguay climbed back to the top of the soccer world.

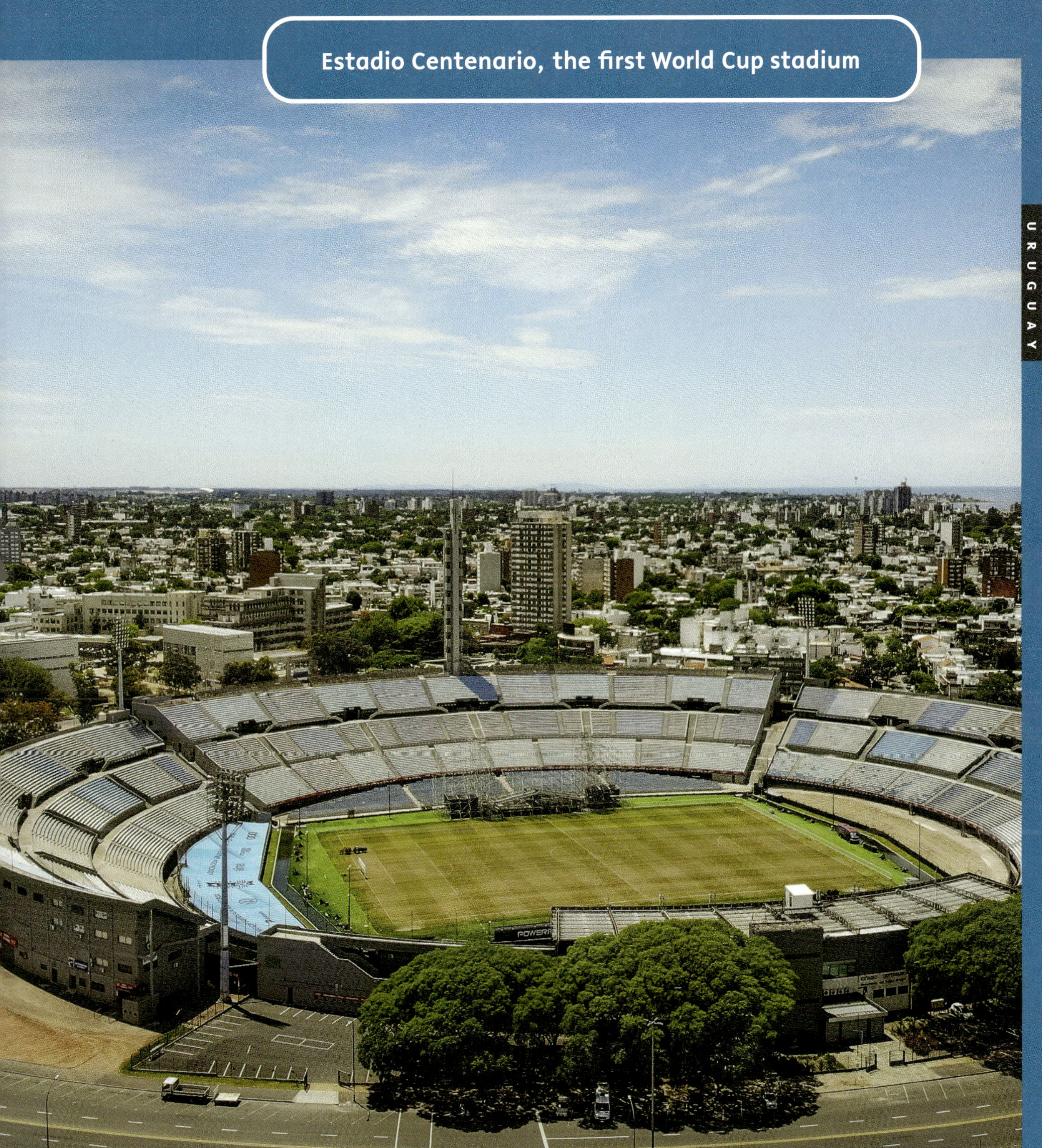

Estadio Centenario, the first World Cup stadium

URUGUAY

The 1950 World Cup winning goal

The 1950 World Cup was held in Brazil. Uruguay reached the final to face the host country at Maracanã Stadium. Brazil was a huge **favorite** in the match. Uruguay was down 1–0 at halftime. But it came back in the second half to win 2–1. It was one of the biggest surprise wins in soccer history. The match became known as the "Maracanazo" (the "Maracanã Smash"). The small country upset its much bigger neighbor.

Team Stars

Uruguay has had many great stars in its history. Héctor Scarone helped Uruguay to Olympic victories and their first World Cup. José Leandro Andrade was a key member of the same teams. He was the first Black soccer player to play in the Olympics. Obdulio Varela captained Uruguay to their 1950 World Cup victory. He was one of the great leaders in the national team.

Defensive midfielder José Leandro Andrade

Striker Luis Suárez

Diego Forlán won the **Golden Ball** at the 2010 World Cup. Diego Godín was one of the best defenders of his generation. He started in 161 matches for Uruguay. **Striker** Luis Suárez is the top goalscorer in Uruguay national team history. Midfielder Federico Valverde is one of the team's best players today. Fans hope he can help bring another World Cup to Uruguay soon.

About the Uruguay National Team

First year: 1902

Team colors: sky blue, white

Home stadium: Estadio Centenario

WORLD CUP VICTORIES:

1930, 4–2 over Argentina

1950, 2–1 over Brazil

WEBSITE:

https://www.auf.org.uy/

Glossary

favorite—a team that is expected to win

Golden Ball—an award given to the best player in the World Cup

rival—a team that plays extra hard against another team

striker—a player who mainly attacks and scores goals, rather than defends

underdog—a team that is not expected to win

The Uruguay national team celebrates a goal.

Index